t u e s d a y s;
a poetic anthology of nature

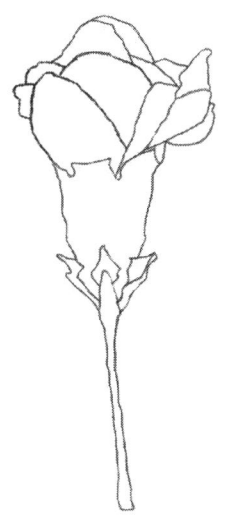

b. gurr

©2020 KAH Publishing LLC & Author
All rights reserved. No part of this publication may be reproduced, stored in a retrieval system or transmitted in any form or by any means electronic, mechanical, photocopying, recording or otherwise without the prior written permission of KAH Publishing LLC &/or the Author except for the use of brief quotations without prior written permission from the publisher &/or author.

ISBN: 9798640324556

b. gurr
@lovebdotme
b.gurr@kahpublishing.com
www.loveb.me

contact@kahpublishing.com
www.kahpublishing.com
www.kahpublishing.com/b-gurr/

for the one who calls me a fucking work of art;
& the one we made.

you have my soul
like a body of water
i lost control
of my mind
when we bet it all
on this love
but it's been divine

love,
b. gurr

INDEX
MIND

```
ORANGE . . . . . . . . . . . . . . 8
ABYSS . . . . . . . . . . . . . . 10
REBUILD . . . . . . . . . . . . . 12
SWIMMING . . . . . . . . . . . . .14
STATIC . . . . . . . . . . . . . .16
SHADOW . . . . . . . . . . . . . .18
PENANCE . . . . . . . . . . . . . 20
LOVER. . . . . . . . . . . . . . .22
THROAT . . . . . . . . . . . . . .24
COFFINS . . . . . . . . . . . . . 26
HEADSCAPE. . . . . . . . . . . . .28
FEARS. . . . . . . . . . . . . . .30
(NOT) SORRY . . . . . . . . . . . 32
PAPER. . . . . . . . . . . . . . .34
BIRTHED . . . . . . . . . . . . . 36
HEAL . . . . . . . . . . . . . . .38
HOW. . . . . . . . . . . . . . . .40
BLOOM . . . . . . . . . . . . . . 42
WALNUT . . . . . . . . . . . . . .44
POETRY . . . . . . . . . . . . . .46
FIND. . . . . . . . . . . . . . . 48
WORDS. . . . . . . . . . . . . . .50
CRY . . . . . . . . . . . . . . . 52
WANT . . . . . . . . . . . . . . .54
MADNESS . . . . . . . . . . . . . 56
LML. . . . . . . . . . . . . . . .58
WORTHY. . . . . . . . . . . . . . 60
CLANDESTINELY. . . . . . . . . . .62
BE . . . . . . . . . . . . . . . .64
PETALS . . . . . . . . . . . . . .66
JOY . . . . . . . . . . . . . . . 68
MOMMA. . . . . . . . . . . . . . .70
FLOWERS. . . . . . . . . . . . . .72
ORCHID. . . . . . . . . . . . . . 74
GREW. . . . . . . . . . . . . . . 76
HIKE . . . . . . . . . . . . . . .78
LYING. . . . . . . . . . . . . . .80
GARDEN. . . . . . . . . . . . . . 82
WITCH. . . . . . . . . . . . . . .84
DREAM. . . . . . . . . . . . . . .86
COLD. . . . . . . . . . . . . . . 88
MOOD . . . . . . . . . . . . . . .90
HER. . . . . . . . . . . . . . . .92
AFRAID . . . . . . . . . . . . . .94
```

BODY

```
ONCE . . . . . . . . . . . . . . .  98
DEW . . . . . . . . . . . . . . . 100
KEY . . . . . . . . . . . . . . . 102
TULIP . . . . . . . . . . . . . . 104
WILT . . . . . . . . . . . . . . .106
LIPS . . . . . . . . . . . . . . .108
CACTUS . . . . . . . . . . . . . .110
BONES . . . . . . . . . . . . . . 112
SKIN . . . . . . . . . . . . . . .114
BELONG . . . . . . . . . . . . . .116
BEAUTIFUL . . . . . . . . . . . . 118
DANDELION . . . . . . . . . . . . 120
POISE . . . . . . . . . . . . . . 122
PUSSY . . . . . . . . . . . . . . 124
DIVINE . . . . . . . . . . . . . .126
TASTE . . . . . . . . . . . . . . 128
BODY. . . . . . . . . . . . . . . 130
DANCING . . . . . . . . . . . . . 132
HEAD . . . . . . . . . . . . . . .134
HOME . . . . . . . . . . . . . . .136
DUST. . . . . . . . . . . . . . . 138
WILDPHIRE . . . . . . . . . . . . 140
STROKE . . . . . . . . . . . . . .142
SHIP . . . . . . . . . . . . . . .144
LOVE . . . . . . . . . . . . . . .146
SWELLS . . . . . . . . . . . . . .148
HAZE . . . . . . . . . . . . . . .150
LET . . . . . . . . . . . . . . . 152
WASTE . . . . . . . . . . . . . . 154
AGLOW . . . . . . . . . . . . . . 156
ACHE . . . . . . . . . . . . . . .158
FLAVOUR . . . . . . . . . . . . . 160
VIBRANT. . . . . . . . . . . . . .162
BLUR . . . . . . . . . . . . . . .164
DRUGS. . . . . . . . . . . . . . .166
AMAZING. . . . . . . . . . . . . .168
TUF . . . . . . . . . . . . . . . 170
DEEP . . . . . . . . . . . . . . .172
DIME . . . . . . . . . . . . . . .174
IF . . . . . . . . . . . . . . . .176
FIFTY . . . . . . . . . . . . . . 178
WINE . . . . . . . . . . . . . . .180
OVERFLOWINGLY . . . . . . . . .  182
```

SOUL

GRACE	186
KINETIC	188
CANDLE	190
VELVET	192
MOON	194
MORE	196
TRUE	198
STARDUST	200
FIRE	202
BUILD	204
9/5	206
FOREVER	208
MAGIC	210
SEED	212
ZODIAC	214
UNDERTOW	216
UNICORN	218
FEEL	220
KINTSUGI	222
NEVER	224
FOUND	226
RAINIER	228
VOILETS	230
ECLIPSE	232
GODDESS	234
HELD	236
NEVERLAND	238
TAUGHT	240
SLEEP	242
YOU	244
UP	246
RUSH	248
STARS	250
HALF	252
TITANIC	254
SOUL	256
COEXIST	258
LOSE	260
RAINBOWS	262
SIGN	264
FLOOD	266
DESTINED	268
GOODNIGHT	270

introduction:

    the title of this book came about while reflecting on what the major moments that my life shared. phone calls from my estranged father when i was a young child. story time at my local library. family jazz nights at ikea, where us kids ate free. weekly girls nights as an adult. the day i met the love of my life. our tuesday night dates. these events brought me growth shaping much of who i am today: mind, body & soul.

    i started writing poetry at age 11 as a way to transmute my feelings; similar to one would with a journal, but in a way that was veiled with analogies & multiple meanings. i needed this puzzle to give myself both security & protection from my parents, & later an abusive ex-partner. whether i was experiencing something that i wanted to remember forever, or pain i wanted to transmute into healing, writing poetry, even just in my head til i can get to a pen. poetry became a form of self therapy for me at a young age. in particularly traumatic situations i've always found an escape in counting syllables & building rhymes in my head, til it was safe to be in my body again. later, my soul transmutes those all those memories from my mind & body, into healing. into life. into love. poetry became a place where alchemy exists, & i could communicate with the universe.

    at barely 14 years of age, i had a severely massive stroke. only a year earlier, my first poem was published & i was growing in the confidence that i could dream big. now suddenly i was forced to re-learn nearly everything; walking, talking, writing, eating, chewing, buttons, you name it. it was hard to face these challenges lacking any feeling of control. i escaped again into my poetry, & grew to learn a new way to live life that has stuck with me into adulthood. both my childhood & early 20's saw a lot of trauma & abuse. my body had responded with several life threatening issues that had me looking at an expiration date of 31 years old. the age i am now.

    i turned my life upside down, in an effort to save it & had an extremely risky & rare surgery. it was successful, & in facing a lengthy recovery time i decided to start building the foundation of my new life. i went back to college, adopted a puppy, traveled, acquired my dream job, but in the midst of all that, i wrote. i dove into art, because poetry has more forms than language alone. i decided to live my life in a way that would inspire love & creativity in myself & those around me. i committed to organically facilitating my passion for poetry, regardless of where it went. i experienced wounds heal & dreams come alive. ultimately, the act of staying true to myself & my art, drastically altered the path of what i thought that looked like. from falling in love with my muse to becoming a mother, this journey has broken open & reassembled every part of me. it has humbled me & unearthed a deeper understanding of the intricacies of the nature of the universe.

    i'm learning to channel energy, create alchemy & raise the frequency of my reality & those around me. to me, that is poetry.

    i hope that what you read resonates with you & you feel a connection to the energy infused within & above all, you experience a knowing that you too, can find healing & power in the self expression of art.

love, b.

the poems contained in each collection were categorized
in accordance with the energy of healing, watering, &
growing with this part of myself.

tuesdays;
MIND

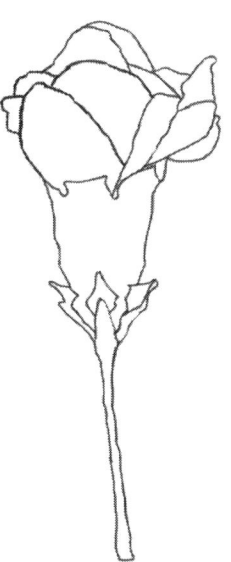

b. gurr

ORANGE

a citrus rose   burning orange
memories built   burnt in storage
come to light feeling foreign
blooms in a frame
lost in a maze
above flowers
in flames
& below pink tinted clouds
i never
heard fire
this loud
she burns
for the truth
& she burns
proud

// © b. gurr

ABYSS

an abyss in this place
she's deep as the ocean
y'all just exist in this space
sleepin' on the erosion

// © b. gurr

REBUILD

all i know is falling
apart so tragically
but isn't that how we grow
so we can rebuild
what's been shattered

// © b. gurr

SWIMMING

all i want is the sun on your face
swimming in your eyes
this wasn't meant to be a race
tell me no more lies

// © b. gurr

STATIC

been here half my life
lonely islands & love shacks
not waiting on you

standing on a mountain top
lava seeping through the cracks
i'm static
do you hear me
quietly crackling
like the fire i left our memories in

let your tears sink into the seas
hurl your fears into the sun
let be what may be
wheat laden breezes, i never won

it's too heavy heavy heavy
on my chest
this love got me fucked up
you're not like the rest

// © b. gurr

S H A D O W

feelin' proud how can i miss
when these clouds be lookin' like this
when the moon got my back like glue
cause that's what shadows do

// © b. gurr

PENANCE

fragile resilience
you are my penance
we killed forever

// © b. gurr

LOVER

from the eye of the tiger
sweet coastal blooms
tumbling salt water
rainbow cascades blue
melting sunset golden lover

// © b. gurr

T H R O A T

he reached for the flowers
the words she was saying
as they peaked out her throat

he wanted her powers
but she was not playing
the magic was in her note

at the top of her tower
you can find her praying
every word she ever wrote

// © b. gurr

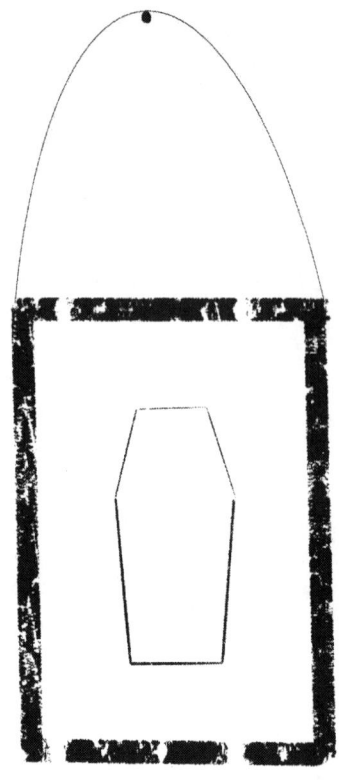

COFFINS

he swore the land was level
& she believed him
so they built a home
with all the little things
from the ground up
with walls made of resolve
& a roof tiled with kind words
they hung little memories of joy all around
but there was nothing underneath
only a hole
with otherwise empty coffins
containing respect
& desire

// © b. gurr

HEADSCAPE

headscape looking like blooms
torn at the seams like petals
landspace feeling like you
shifting tectonic plates like metals

// © b. gurr

FEARS

her love fed him
through the tears

his passion starved her
feeding her fears

// © b. gurr

(NOT) SORRY

i'm saddened that my fire
has turned your heart cold

i'm saddened that demanding equal rights
is an idea that still needs sold

i'm saddened that the sensuality of my light
be something you avoid like the common cold

i'm saddened that me being bi
made us friends only of old

i'm saddened that allying to human rights
you view as being bold

i'm saddened that you hung me out to dry
because i was something you couldn't control

i'm saddened you've turned a blind eye
& it's not something i'd have foretold

i'm saddened but hear me when i sigh
that you too my dear, yourself are gold

& if perhaps one day you'd like to try
to lean into love & grow

it would be an honor most high
to witness your blooms unfold

// © b. gurr

PAPER

hold the cold cut diamond
& windy white veil
i'm the type to prefer your mind
& hand cut paper in the mail

// © b. gurr

BIRTHED

how are you really mine
i birthed you into the light
& a dream overtook my life

// © b. gurr

37

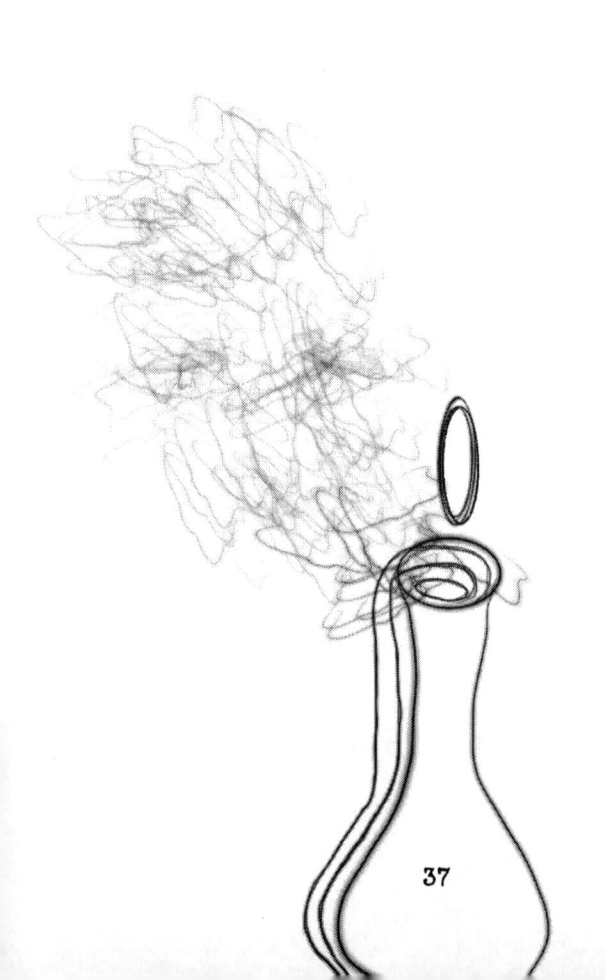

H E A L

if words could heal wounds
then poetry is the potion
the burns would peel plumes
some quietly & some spoken
let's affirm good with surreal moons
& all agree we have emotion
that births full feel blooms
as vocally as the ocean

// © b. gurr

H O W

how often i mistook
being someone's   fantasy
for someone's d
            r
               e
                  a
                     m

// © b. gurr

B L O O M

i know i can't give you what you want
tell me what to do
i know i'm giving you all of what you don't want
this all happened too soon

but did you ever think of me
i won't bleed for you
did you ever think of how it could be
it's so quiet in this room

it won't be for long
for longer than i've loved you
i have to be strong
stronger for this piece of you

there is an entire universe inside me
a universe made up of pieces left by you
what will be will be
but i choose to bloom

pick off my petals
try as you might
my world is run by rebels
who
don't
sleep
at

n
i
g
h
t

// © b. gurr

WALNUT

i painted on his back what i saw in him

a tree with many circles marking his time here

like wisdom under his eyes more beautiful

with every new growth strong enough to carry

pain of death every autumn & come back to life every spring

i gave him fruit for the brain & a shell for safety

i scratched out roots with purpose but wild & winding so that
           maybe
           he
           would
           feel
           those
           things

// © b. gurr

POETRY

if my art were a potion
you brought poetry into motion
with the drop of an ocean
love, or some such notion

// © b. gurr

47

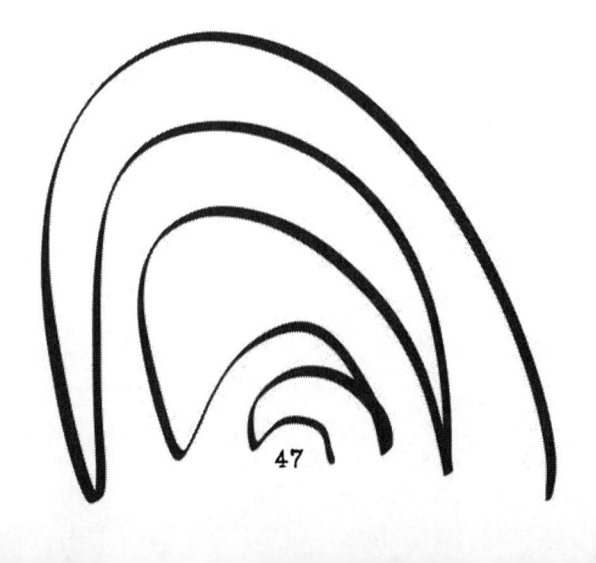

F I N D

how can you let go
of someone you can't find
irreplaceable castle made of snow
you tell me it's all in my mind
a love you do not know
lurking in between the lines
each colour of the rainbow
saturated & defined

// © b. gurr

WORDS

in my dreams
you hold my face
& kiss my neck
tell me words i can't forget

// © b. gurr

CRY

it's not the little girl i used to be
that's crying
it's me
crying
for the little girl that i used to be

// © b. gurr

W A N T

liking the i d e a
of having something
is n o t the same
as wanting it

// © b. gurr

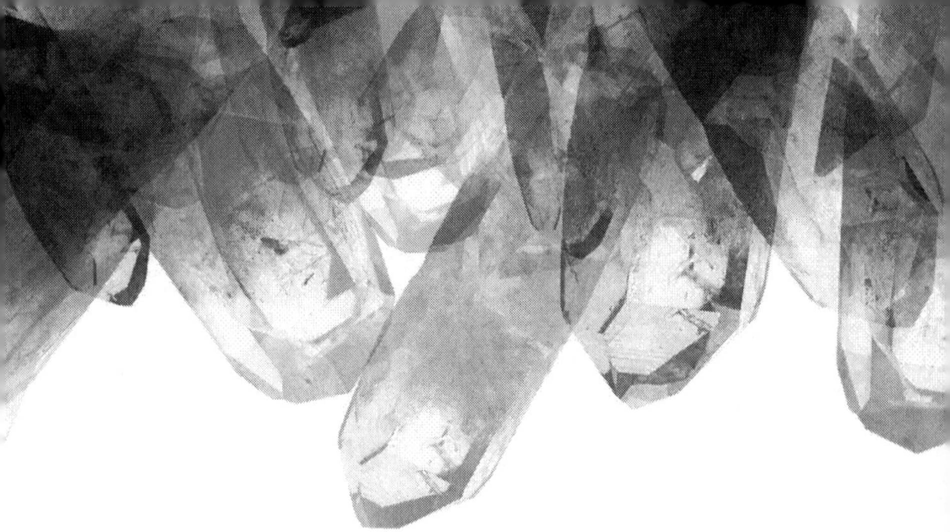

MADNESS

love is
madness
& i am
m a d
about   y o u

// © b. gurr

LML

love me like
read my rhymes
& love me like
it's the last time
to love me like
it's your right
so love me like
all fucks no fights
you love me like
taste my light
& love me like
you just might
love me like
it could put you in psych
to love me like
straight jacket hold me tight
love me like
black & white
& love me like
a hunger strike
for love me like
the last bite
of love me like
a never ending appetite
or love me like
the sun burns bright
but love me like
you won't go blind
so love me like
by feeling not by sight
& love me like
my starry knight
to love me like
in another life
just love me like
we reunite

// © b. gurr

WORTHY

my prayer
is that each woman
within you
always knows
she is worthy

// © b. gurr

CLANDESTINELY

pour it out you're in too deep
choking from the inside
your shadow follows me

words as sweet as my skin
consume me whole before we begin

i see worlds upon worlds in you
collide against my stars
encrust yourself in floating jewel dust
i sailed too far

salt water dripping from my lips
your eyes are sirens of the sea
drown me with your sound
sand on my knees, i beg clandestinely

seaweed & sunflowers live in your head
close your eyelids before i jump in
that green abyss is beckoning
take my life in your wave

// © b. gurr

BE

she asked her lover was he busy was he maybe free
'no' he said 'but please- tell me what you thirst'
'i want to be wanted' she said 'have fun & just be'
he took a breath & sipped his coffee
'go for it' he told her

// © b. gurr

PETALS

she bloomed
in a patch of weeds
forgiving those that choked her, still
with all of her colour

so they cut her down
stuck her in a vase
& gave her away

she stretched towards the sun
cause that's how flowers survive
but without water
she drowned in open air

so with a satin ribbon
she hung upon the wall
dancing
as she fell apart

a pile of petals
on hard cold tile

he gathered them up
dusted his bed with her
& basked in her bouquet

his sweat
her tears
their blood
would bring her back to life

// © b. gurr

J O Y

someone who is not acquainted with happiness
will question anyone who lives it
unaware that
u n a t t a c h m e n t
radical acceptance
constant gratitude
& unconditional love
are the source
regardless of
circumstances
& that is where true j o y lies

// © b. gurr

MOMMA

sometimes i wonder
if she misses me
but then again
how can you miss someone
you never wanted to know
so i sing judy garland
under the light of the stove
as i swirl to the memory of
that perfect gene kelly harmony
imagining a feeling that never existed

// © b. gurr

F L O W E R S

standing in a field
taking in the flowers
never lost among the reeds
cause shorty's got powers
enough to see through
that she'll never be
the one that you value
more than the beauty
of all of the what ifs
& the others you search
while you say i'm your pick
but not of this earth
& maybe that's why
i feel alone in the rain
i've already died
stuck in a frame
a moment in time
only myself to blame
they never want
what they can have
they'd rather a bitch they can flaunt
than a queen who can nav
through life's ups & downs
when they feeling low
now who's the clown
& who killed this flow
like the damn, on the river
that nourishes & grows
the roots beneath her
& the petals that blow
in the wind where you live
that never seems to still
always so active
& strong in your will
to be free to roam
among the flora forever
& pop up in poems
regardless of weather

// © b. gurr

ORCHID

suspended in space

p u l l i n g t h e t i d e

in that endless blue place

s t i l l i n t h e q u i e t

not too far, just offshore

b l o o m s a w i n d c h i l l e d o r c h i d

wanting only l o v e not war

'a flower that blooms in the dark'
she heard the moon say
leaves a lot more question marks
than a flower that thrives in the day

but the m o o n could not see

the light he shone

from worlds beyond the s e a

for this orchid, alone

// © b. gurr

G R E W

why do i pour myself into you
i think i see in you someone i used to
know a long long time ago
perhaps under the sea
or on a planet named rainier
but somehow i know you & it makes me cry
because why would my soul recognize
maybe i'll know in another life
in another time
a different timeline
but this time we found
a piece of ourselves in each other
i grew those pieces
can we live another
life in peace
just know i saw your eyes
& i knew
how little i really knew
when you showed me you
thought you'd scare me
but you don't really know me
underneath it all i know you feel me
you could have all of me
all the parts no one has seen
i can't help but think
that if you dove into me
really real just be
you would find that piece
of us from another time
go back & rewind
cause i still remember that time
you grabbed my face looked me in the eyes
& said i don't know how or why
but you've got me & the jokes on you
i thought to myself how or why
would i ever keep a beautiful soul like you
so i made art of you
cause that's what i saw in you
still do it's true
all the mess
all the best

// © b. gurr

H I K E

you better get going
this forecast be lookin like
it'll be snowing
way up there way up high
737 high like boeing

cause lately you been sayin
that you're fresh outta fucks
but really you been playin
boo, you fresh outta luck

so go find some dirts to hike
oh baby might i suggest
you go find some skirts to hike
glad i got that off my chest

you've been dismissed
can't say you'll be missed

i'ma find someone
who'll get dirty with me
ima find someone
who'll get flirty with me

// © b. gurr

L Y I N G

there was this place
inside her head
where she kept space
for memories of words he said
gently, closely, as he lay
lying, in her bed

// © b. gurr

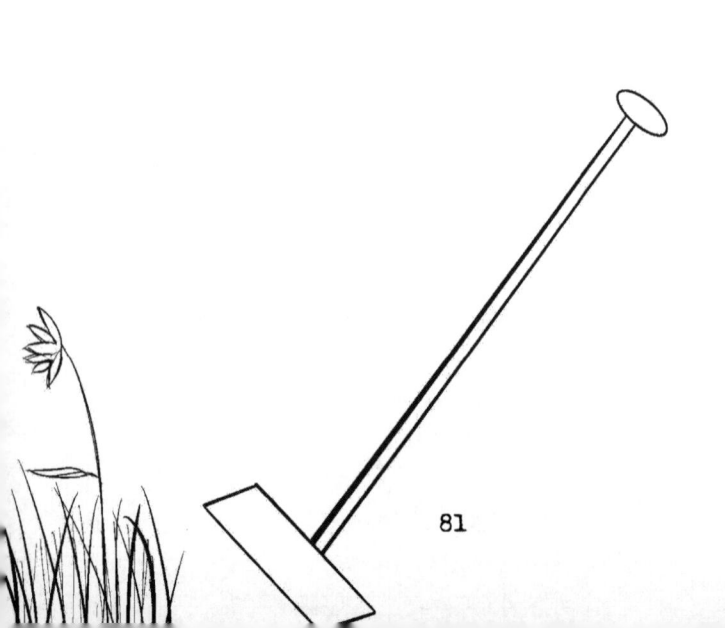

GARDEN

there's a castle within your mind
where all you've ever wanted
collides with everything
you never thought you'd have
i find myself in the gap between
so tell me
am i filling in
or do i fill you up
cause i have
too much to give
too far to grow
to let it waste
down the cracks
between the bricks
you built so high
around your kingdom
but what's a king without a queen
what's a castle without a garden
so dig your heels in
& dig your fears up
my soul lives below, can you hear her?
quietly shuffling through the earth
beneath your feet
she's not a side hoe
she's the whole damn garden
she's the moss growing up the wall
just to soften your climb
she's the ivy growing over
to cling to when you lose your grip
she's the strawberries covering the ground
to break the blow should you fall
she's the oak you can hide in
a shelter in the storm
& she's the flowers all around
weaving in & out
to spray colour in every direction
& clean the air you breathe
all she requires is light

// © b. gurr

W I T C H

when i was young
my momma would say in truth
things not so kind
'you must be a witch
girl quiet your tongue
questioning ones like you
have spirits in their mind
& who's to say which is which'

// © b. gurr

D R E A M

when left to my own devices
i allow myself to dream
when all that's left are vices
& nothing's as it seems

neither clear nor concise
messily stitched at every seam
presumably not list price
missing that new mint gleam

ready to be packed on ice
dying alive ima crab in steam
wanna see the northern lights
& slow churn soft ice cream

so much has been sacrificed
by everyone on the team
not allowed to socialize
do i whisper or do i scream

now's the time to mobilize
gotta keep swimming upstream
only the strong willed survive
& allow themselves to dream

// © b. gurr

C O L D

where are you
somewhere in your feelings
thought we got through
but here we are reeling
didn't i tell you

i was stuck, frozen
dying
but not dead
i reached out, crying
but you left me on read
i never stopped trying
you never heard a word i said

what was i to do
where was i to go
i only wanted you
but you were just so cold

// © b. gurr

M O O D

in times of solitude
will is subdued
we strip ourselves
of distraction
the real you
will debut
we find ourselves
shit's never done
keep ourselves renewed
now that's a mood

// © b. gurr

H E R

you look at me with fear
not knowing what i'll take next
your love, my dear
or your breath

a wild thing can't be stopped
flying fast & free
runaway horse
you can't bridle me

prints of where we were
stamped into the sand
you think i'm her
i stop as you start to stand

if sand is time
& time is money
fuck this rhyme
& be here with me

// © b. gurr

A F R A I D

you see, when he touched me
it was in such a way
that i couldn't tell if he was afraid
of destroying me
or afraid
of me

// © b. gurr

tuesdays;
BODY

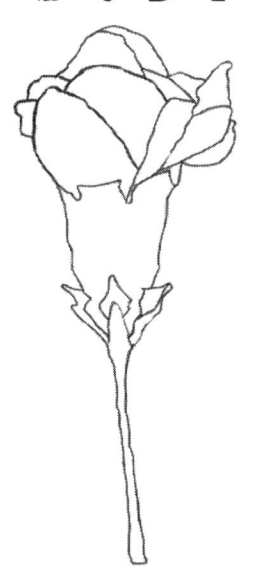

b. gurr

O N C E

```
    some beers
     a smile
     a wink
     a slice
he grabbed my hand
 i rolled the dice
  he told me once
  he took me twice
 said he never once
   had it so nice
```

// © b. gurr

DEW

my blossom awaits
the sunrise for a taste
of your morning dew

// © b. gurr

K E Y

in your hands you hold a key
searching for any lock in which to park
not the kind of lock to have to keep
but somewhere still & quiet in the dark
just something to pick, nothing too deep

but magic keys have magic locks
& if you look, you will find
that in my hands i hold a box
unlatched, but for you confined

did you think the lock would be gold
like those medals begot of war
precious, gleaming, sterile & cold
or did you imagine something on a door
dirty but polished, ornate & bold

no, this lock is solid platinum
smart, clean, smooth & versatile
not the problem but still not the sum
for gold is soft & melts in fires
so take your key, pulchrum magnum
try this lock, you don't need wires
insert firmly, turning slowly, feel me come
to life for you only, breathe & respire

// © b. gurr

T U L I P

in the silence at night
you might hear the shuffle
a crimson tulip, pulling in tight
the taste of truffle

// © b. gurr

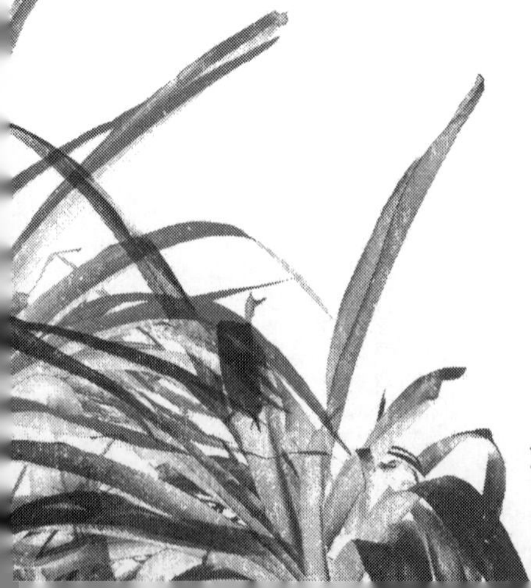

WILT

if the light you seek
to soak up
into each vein of your blossom
is running away from you
over the horizon
do not keep reaching
for eventually
you will have bent
so far past
a lilt
you will have
wasted your reach
a withering wilt

// © b. gurr

LIPS

if only
you knew
how many times
i wrote i love you
on your back
with my
lips

// © b. Gurr

CACTUS

if it's dessert you after no lie
this wild cactus
known to get you high
all frills no fuss
the desert supplies
a place where such
thirst thrives

so this idea you've planted
tight between my thighs
really lacks enchantment
& it is bound to die
in the flood with abandon
exotic & rare i defy
the fruit of the plantain
beyond this sky

// © b. gurr

BONES

i heard bricks made better homes
than weak old bones
but what if that's just mistrust
'cause it all turns to dust

// © b. gurr

S K I N

i get this feeling that feels like home
when i go to the ocean
so what is running through your veins

down to my skin let us begin
down to your skin, skin so clear
i can see right through you
can you see into me?

through my sea drenched freckles
into the depths & onto the shores
where washed up hopes lay
sun-dried, but not forgotten

find my sandy feet with yours
wrap yourself around me
whisper my name slowly
kill me softly

salt in my eyes
be my burial ground
someone is praying for you
crying out with bated breath
between your sheets

// © b. gurr

BELONG

i belong to the s e a
d
e
e
p
& vast
her goddess grew inside me
giving more than i could ever have asked

// © b. gurr

BEAUTIFUL

i believed you when you said last
that i was beautiful, no quips
because two whole summers had passed
without those words leaving your lips

// © b. gurr

D A N D E L I O N

i am a dandelion
growing where i can
sometimes
all over
the place
so you can choose to see a flower
or you can choose to see a weed
darling, i'll b l o o m all the same
but when my time has come
don't close me into a book
to sit & look pretty
keep me f r e e
& watch my creation
petals taken in the w i n d
sprouting fresh
seedlings
to grow anew

// © b. gurr

POISE

i always had a thing for curly haired boys
with charm, wit
style & poise

but never have i known a man such as you
with heart, soul
decency & truth

// © b. gurr

P U S S Y

his eyes were no longer dim
'your pussy is heaven'
he continued
'it always has been'

// © b. gurr

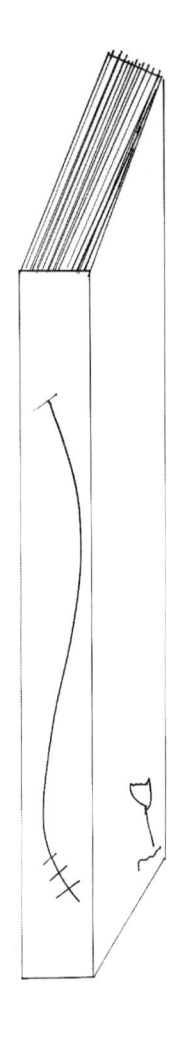

DIVINE

her fears she kept
stacked in her spine
her tears she wept
rather too much at times
her love was inept
really but rather divine
the way she stepped
lively as moonshine

// © b. gurr

TASTE

he walked through the door
saw me sitting there
& got on his knees

without a word or what for
gently pushed me into the chair
& tasted the inside of me

// © b. gurr

B O D Y

he ran
fingers over me
like a rainstorm

he slipped
both arms around
over & under
like a wave

he took
all of me
body & soul
like a flood

// © b. gurr

DANCING

lightyears beyond
might just go blonde
from the bleach of the sun
i'm preachin' for one
but counting the stars
just as if they were ours
to reign in a crown
before they rain down
to prove that all light
returns to dust despite
our efforts in vain
against gravity, with pain
but the soul will live on
til infinity & beyond
molding pieces of the mind
holding, it releases over time
so fill your soul up
to the brim of the cup
with kindness & love
the stuff gratitude is made of
in abundance, of blessings
we're all star dust dancing
we just call it something fancy

// © b. gurr

HEAD

he lived inside her head
deep inside
saying words never said

he lived inside her head
in the back behind
soft, wet, warm & red

he lived inside her head
late nights
on the edge of the bed

// © b. gurr

H O M E

falling asleep on me
aw ain't that sweet
naw, not really
because you see
you haven't seen me
you be gazin' at screens
hugging my knee
why do you feel
so far from me
i'm far from home
far too often far too long
since i been to the ocean
oh shit
you are my home
but you far too
without you
i just got mountains blue
you know, waves times two
so before you
& i guess now too
i'm drifting into the sea
until you come to me
without the moon & the sea
i die my soul ceases
& now i know what's been
killing me
it's the sea
far from me
far from home
i need you like i need
the sea
can i run into you
before i turn blue
or should i run into
the ocean blue

// © b. gurr

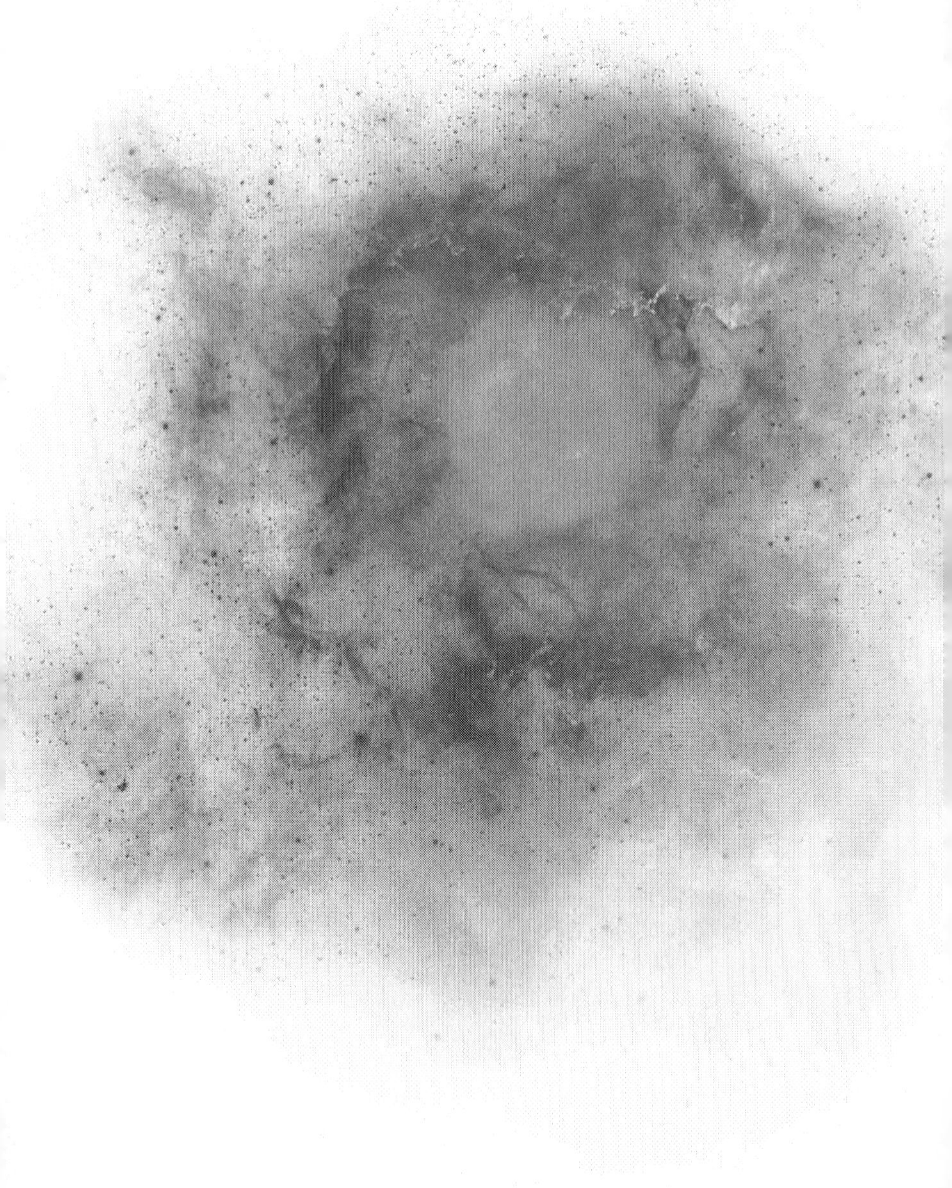

D U S T

everyone prays to a god
in the silence or aloud
in a churchyard
or crying out to stars
cosmic dust
i'm made of the same stuff
a goddess she
got you on your knees

// © b. gurr

WILDPHIRE

i wanna see you shippin'
these winter wildflowers
i think i'm really trippin'
on september sapphires
high dive swimmin'
in those blue flame fire
eyes & i am drownin'
in your wildfire
i got holy water drippin'
from that rectifier
i never wanna stop sippin'
you really that fire
i won't be dippin'
no qualifier
i think you must be trippin'
to think there's someone flyer
high key no clippin'
a wild flower
i'll always meet
your highest higher
i'll always be
your wildflower

// © b. gurr

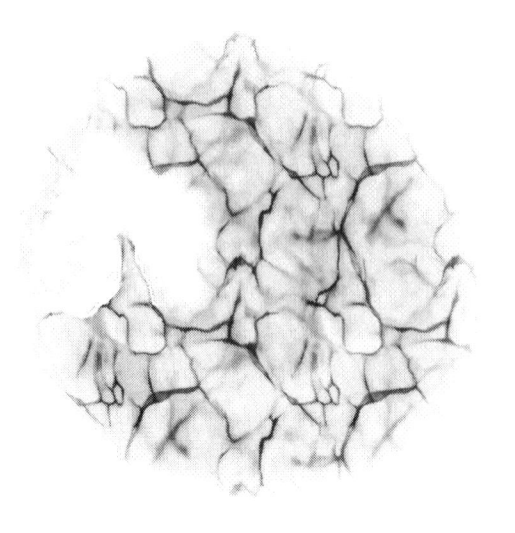

S T R O K E

a day in the life of this girl in her head
calculating every move leaving much unsaid

when the very blood that kept her alive
came together to spoil & plot
against her life
forming a clot

leaving a hole
in the shape of a heart
flooding her goals
before she could start

adapting to new realities
stronger than she feels
so compromising she deals
with the many insecurities

expecting more from herself
than anyone ever does
she keeps on ignoring her health
for if she responds to the fuzz
she feels or rather puts on a shelf
it may betray her madonnas

// © b. gurr

S H I P

a ship out to sea
is what i fancy myself
a safe place to be
unsinkable, an island unto myself
but if you look closely
i'm just a little sailboat
in an unknown ocean
struggling to stay afloat
see, he is the storm within
still i never bring a coat
because he is also the calm
at the center
a balm
for the pain i suffer
through the qualm
these waves keep lurching me
to & fro
to & fro
him

// © b. gurr

L O V E

loving you
is leaning into the breeze
with the sunset in view

// © b. gurr

SWELLS

my flesh, my skin
swells with she
sparkles ripplin'
the sea
d a n c e s
with me

// © b. gurr

H A Z E

purple haze
each damn day
your jungle eyes
a lush paradise isle

// © b. gurr

L E T

she let the grass grow
& let the flowers wilt
her spirit got tired
from the kingdom she built

// © b. gurr

WASTE

she ran
to escape
the feeling
that somehow
each breath
every touch
was a
colossal waste
for life
is much
too precious
to live
feeling like
second string

// © b. gurr

AGLOW

smooth as ice
white as snow
aspen eyes
brightly aglow

// © b. gurr

A C H E

sometimes i ache
for you
in my bones
like a rainy day
that won't let up
& won't give in

// © b. gurr

F L A V O U R

takes two players
no new playas
only true stargazers
love you lay her
no rude glaciers
clark & lewis trail blazers

gotta shoot like mccollum
on your game, deal, shoe in
got that potpourri poo spray em
gold on gold she the louvre, praise em
complex like raspberry blue flavour
find you but don't betray her

// © b. gurr

VIBRANT

who are you to put me in a corner
vibrant, determined & free
i'm not one to be a scorner
i simply miss you wanting me

// © b. gurr

BLUR

there's a line of girls
& a line of guys
wishing, waiting on her
to just give them a try
even so, still she's sure
that she could never say goodbye
to the only one who stirs
her soul, like a wild cotton sky
entangled in your lips, your body's a blur
as much the same to those she denies
be fearless, be still, truly see her
& witness the magic when your souls collide

// © b. gurr

D R U G S

there's a suitcase by the hall
if my dreams take me nowhere
lookin like vintage white walls
real leather gold hardware
i am always ready to fall
inside out of anywhere
alice wonderland space balls
orange bottles full of air
collecting dust like my dolls
blooms of ganja purple hairs
white pills lookin like warhol
cannot beat this love affair
locked inside beneath it all
words on paper, disrepair
you scribbled down a wormhole
they are drugs baby care bear
strongest i have, outta all y'alls
love's a drug & it ain't fair

// © b. gurr

AMAZING

i see blooms in your brain
it's a maze in here
floating flowers aflame
it's amazing here

// © b. gurr

T U F

tough as the thoughts you feel
power in the wrongs we heal
love's the only way that's real

// © b. gurr

D E E P

under the sea
under your wave
it was meant to be
just like this babe

roman goddess of the wide
deep deep blue
you keep me wild
& i'll get you through

// © b. gurr

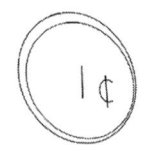

D I M E

dropping a dime
to pick up a penny
is only wasting time
regardless of if you're ready

// © b. gurr

IF

what if you called her

                        b e a u t i f u l

as much as you called her

                                                   o u t

                     b u i l t
                     h e r
                     u p

kissed her

                                               m o u t h

& let her

                    i n t o
                  p l a c e s

                            that no one knew about

        // © b. gurr

FIFTY

with my head in his arms
he looked at me & said
i mean you no harm
when i take others to bed

up here there's you &
then fifty feet of shit
he motioned with his hand
& below is every other bitch

// © b. gurr

W I N E

you don't kiss me anymore
you've been sober for ages
my lips the wine
you've left on the shelf
gathering dust

// © b. gurr

OVERFLOWINGLY

you're here to be
all you've never been
father to be
to she
goddess of the sea
so if you listen closely
she'll tell you love is all we need
that it comes in waves you see
& i must say how lovely
that you've washed over me
perspective & peace
overflowingly
knowing
that not all roads lead
to always happy
or even me
but we're better as we
together us three

// © b. gurr

tuesdays;
SOUL

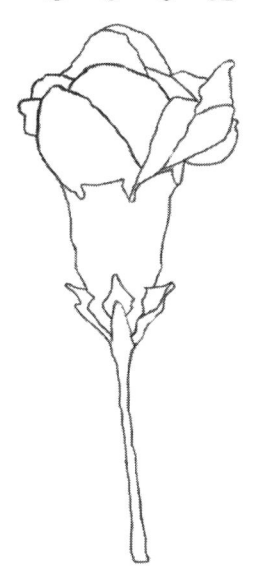

b. gurr

GRACE

you can't expect me
to all of a sudden be
fine with how this feels
if we are really being real
i'm too head over heels
to not know which feelings are real
these things aren't meant to be
toyed with nor raced
not unlike a horse on a sunny day
with something like "the fence" for a name
strapped with a rider who can't hear the bray
so if a bet is what you seek to place
please don't let it be a waste
let it be on love, hope & faith
so that maybe we can live in grace

// © b. gurr

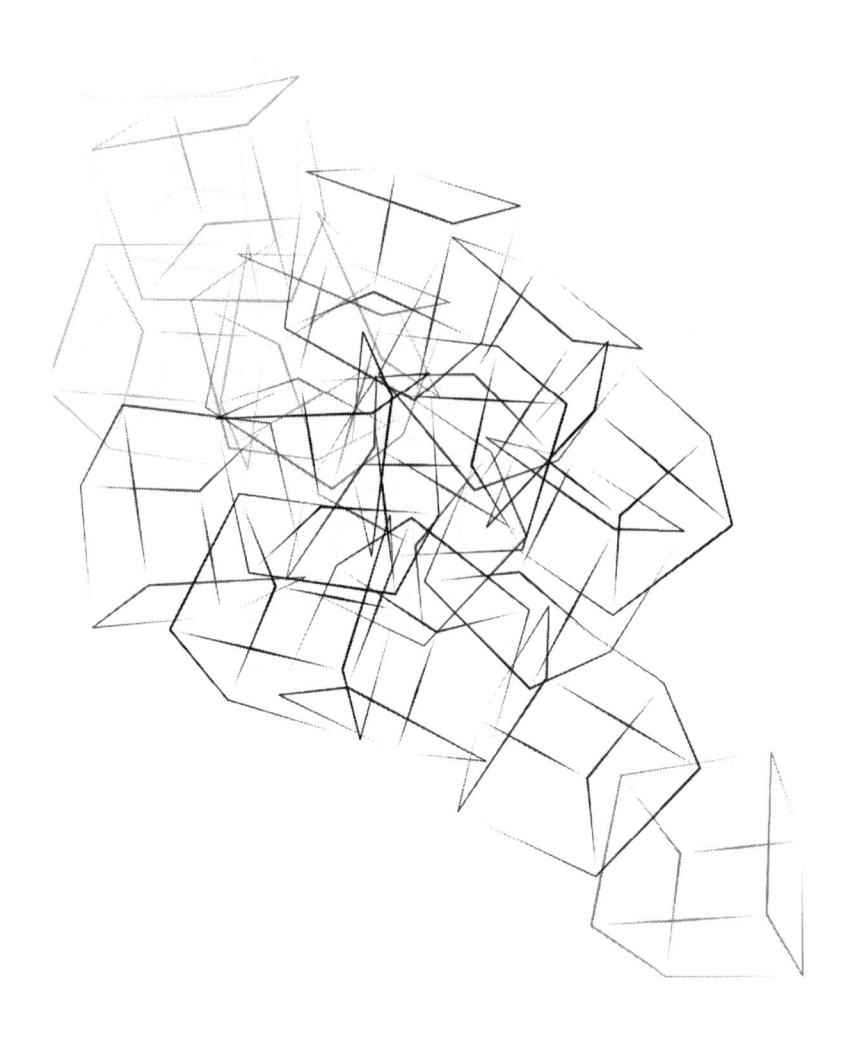

KINETIC

you're electric
you're magnetic
your energy is kinetic
you tell me i can get it

i slide up & down your spine
i could never sacrifice you for lent
your body, your soul, is mine
at least for the moment

you don't know how you say
just haven't figured it out yet
somehow i will, one day
but the jokes on me my pet

money isn't what i'm after
not trying to trap you
don't mistake me for her
let me do what i do

blow your mind & take your heart
fuck you up & tear you apart
ohh so gently at the start
like a thief in the night

pull you in tight
love you? i might.

// © b. gurr

CANDLE

you told her
that she
was
a lot
to handle
so
imagine
how she feels
like a candle
in the wind
hard to contain
a flame so bright

// © b. gurr

VELVET

you held me tight
in all my thorned glory
unafraid of the bite

when i withered
you wept
red

when you bled
i bloomed
red

i couldn't bear your pain
so i found all the strength inside me
my existence, however bane
& bore it in beauty

you taught me that
roses were velvet too

i drop my petals night & day
thorns have marked your face
i didn't need them anyway
to make your world a softer place

// © b. gurr

M O O N

you are the moon
solid & scarred
resisting gravity
pulled into a world
that's spinning
partaking of a light
you do not know
i am the sun
precariously positioned
in your galaxy
one inch closer
everything burns
one inch farther
hell freezes over
so i burn alone
the star that never burns out
when the moon turns their back
the sun shines all the brighter
i keep you warm
for we belong to the same world
you light the places i cannot reach
for an eternity of rotations
i will love you
the way the sun loves the moon
always

// © b. gurr

MORE

you are more
than outer beauty
you are more
than good on your knees
you are more
than the woman they see

// © b. gurr

TRUE

why is it that we doubt
ourselves so much
we fallin outta touch
we told we feel too much
but what if i told you
those feelings are true
they came before you
from the stars to the deep blue
your powers old & new
now look what they do
to your magic, your moon
your light never left you
your shadow is proof

// © b. gurr

STARDUST

whether your core
is pollen or stardust
each stage a line
a vein in every petal
or planet in your system
we must learn
life is in the pause
& all the colour
in between

// © b. gurr

F I R E

we were not born to
f a l l
in love with fire
you see he wanted a
d o l l
but she was not that dire

        half a million meters
            d e e p
      turn   by   turn
      she kept burning bright
      the kind of light you
           k e e p
    the kind that doesn't burn
    the kind that does you right

           but we were not made
    to fall in love with f i r e like that
       so don't let the memories fade
       & remember what love b e g a t

                // © b. gurr

BUILD

we can build something real, grab a glove
beautiful, ours alone, a life anew
founded on gratitude, respect & love
with every fresh dew

// © b. gurr

88

9 / 5

wanted to write
a song just for you
to tell you all of the ways
in which i am grateful for you
but we have a life to live
& it would take the whole damn thing

// © b. gurr

FOREVER

the world's in chaos
my love, so can we
lay here just us
forever please

// © b. gurr

MAGIC

the magic of you & i
we love like we used to
i saw it in your eyes
you felt it too

// © b. gurr

SEED

the earth understands me
she is the womb
for the seed
that is me
i feel myself
shedding
fire
blooms burning

a flower bows
in grace
& beauty
welcoming
the wilt
with the knowledge
that her being
her breath
her beauty
is eternal

a flower's death
is not final
it is simply
the returning of physical form
back into the earth

i return to the mirror
& see the lines on me
the turning of colours
& swaying of my form
the same way

// © b. gurr

Z O D I A C

tell me your sign your zodiac
will reveal more inside track
your stars & moon
my almanac
chakras read
like a paperback
energy don't
lie can't
choke back
intentions you set
that were whack
they say what you give you get back
so baby don't try & back track

// © b. gurr

UNDERTOW

stubborn

        as

            the

                o c e a n

          s t r o n g e r t h a n y o u k n o w

y o u r

              w a v e

          p u l l e d m e i n

                      with the undertow

                            w a s h
                         a s h o r e
                           y o u r
                           f e a r s
                                &
                         d o u b t s

                        i am here

n o t t h e r e

            // © b. gurr

UNICORN

she's a dream girl
unique as a pearl
pure as wild blooms
deep as the wiley blue

// © b. gurr

FEEL

she just wanted to know
& really feel
what it felt like to be loved
through the highs & lows
& really heal
as much as she loved

// © b. gurr

KINTSUGI

she hurled her heart
                      all the little pieces
into the sun

          m o l t e n g o l d
              as it
               s
               a
               n
               k
              into
            t h e s e a

                         knowing the
                           m o o n
                  w o u l d p i e c e

       h e r b a c k t o g e t her
        w   v   by a   e
         a   e   w   v

         // © b. gurr

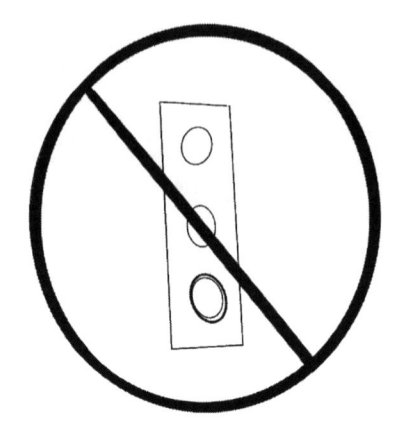

NEVER
go
please

// © b. gurr

FOUND

my person found its soul
my soul found its person

// © b. Gurr

RAINIER

never in my life
until i knew you
was i ever afraid to die

beautiful & blithe
topping the cascades blue
against a clear sunlit sky

// © b. gurr

VIOLETS

my only wish
is to witness
all the violets
that you become

// © b. gurr

ECLIPSE

hold me, hold us tight
you say you can't
you don't know why
in your thoughts
in your feelings too
do or do not
we're alone in this room
i've always known love to hurt
but boy you take the cake
blood, sweat, tears & dirt
whip it up & let it bake
let it sit
then set it on fire
whatever's been writ
in the mud & the mire
i won't fight you
i know how that ends
but i'll fight for us, til i'm blue
like the ocean that exists to mend
shattered sea glass
tossed in so carelessly
with handfuls of ash
by girls who are lonely
can you taste the salt
dripping from my face
does it taste like grace
cause that's all i have for you these days
i don't break but damn, i can bend
over the sun that eclipsed on the day
that i learned your heart was already on lend
lost in the ocean, lost in the spray

// © b. gurr

GODDESS

i'm a life giving goddess
in a broken vessel
i'm a lover of peace
in a ticking time bomb
i'm an ocean
in a drop
i'm a piece of stardust
in a dying cosmos
i'm a balky blossom
in a withering tree
i'm the molten gold
in kintsugi
i'm a burning ember
in a shaded wetland
i'm a river of dreams
that must be damned
you are a fragment
of me

// © b. gurr

H E L D

i'll follow you into the darkness
where i find you in my dreams
there you're lying next to us
& nothings as it seems

there you held me tight
i could feel your breath on my skin
against all odds i slept all night
this once you'd let me in

mercy me i love thee
let's get lost in narnia
here there is no space, there is no time
home in your arms with you in mine

// © b. gurr

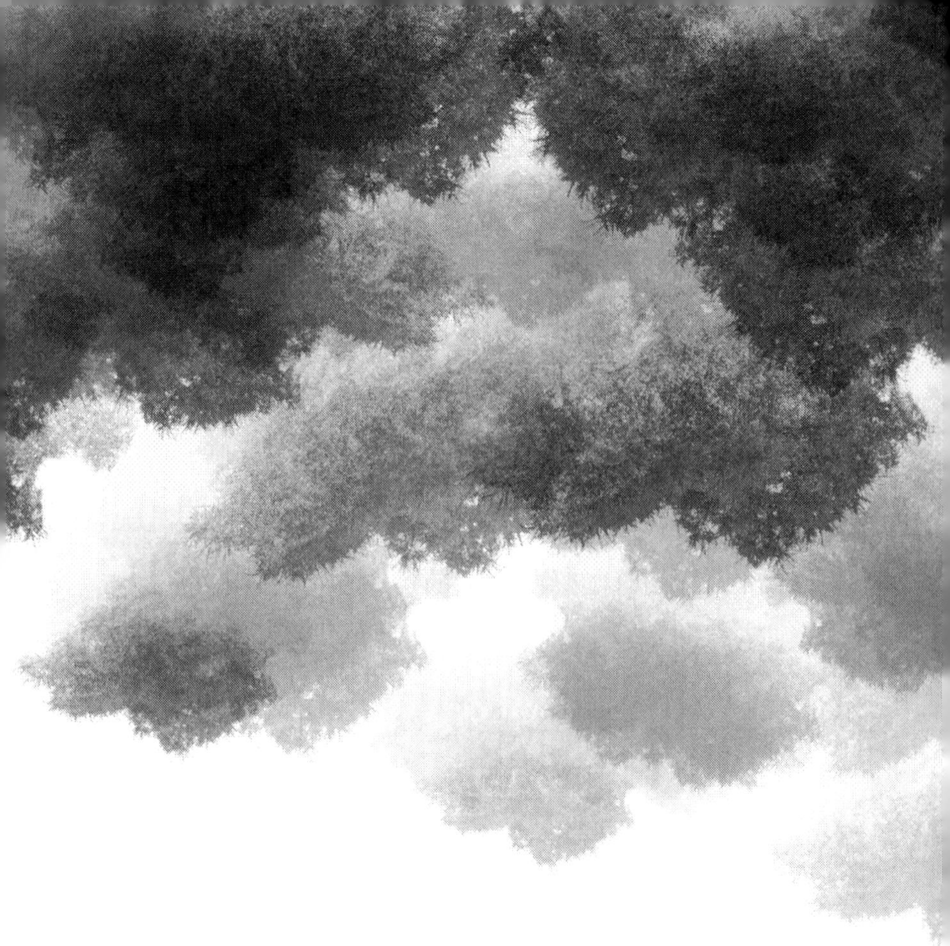

NEVERLAND

i will always kiss you goodbye

for if i see you again, never

until neverland, in clouds so high

i'll hold that feeling forever

i will always kiss you goodnight

for if in your dreams, sailing your ship

to the blue lagoon, above my kite

i'll wake with you still on my lips

// © b. gurr

TAUGHT

i used to be smaller
i used to be taller
i used to be all sorts
of things that didn't line up
with what i was taught
my momma might tell you
my soul has been bought

// © b. gurr

SLEEP

i sleep better touching you
after all you are the moon
there must be something in your blood
pulling me in like the tide brings the mud

// © b. gurr

Y O U

i didn't know
i was sleeping
until you woke me
i didn't know
that i wasn't alive
until you loved me
i didn't know
i was a book
until you read me
i didn't know myself
until you

// © b. gurr

U P

i come from a long line of women
holding men up
who should not have been
held up
but knowing when your kin
need filled up
is not bein' green
it's called a queens cup
her grace ain't convenient
it no start up
she come at it clean
no runner up
she pristine
her tag marked up
not a bone in her mean
she won't be no back up
she grown but not green
shining bright as a buttercup
while the world causes a scene
she pullin' boot straps up
cause she a queen

// © b. gurr

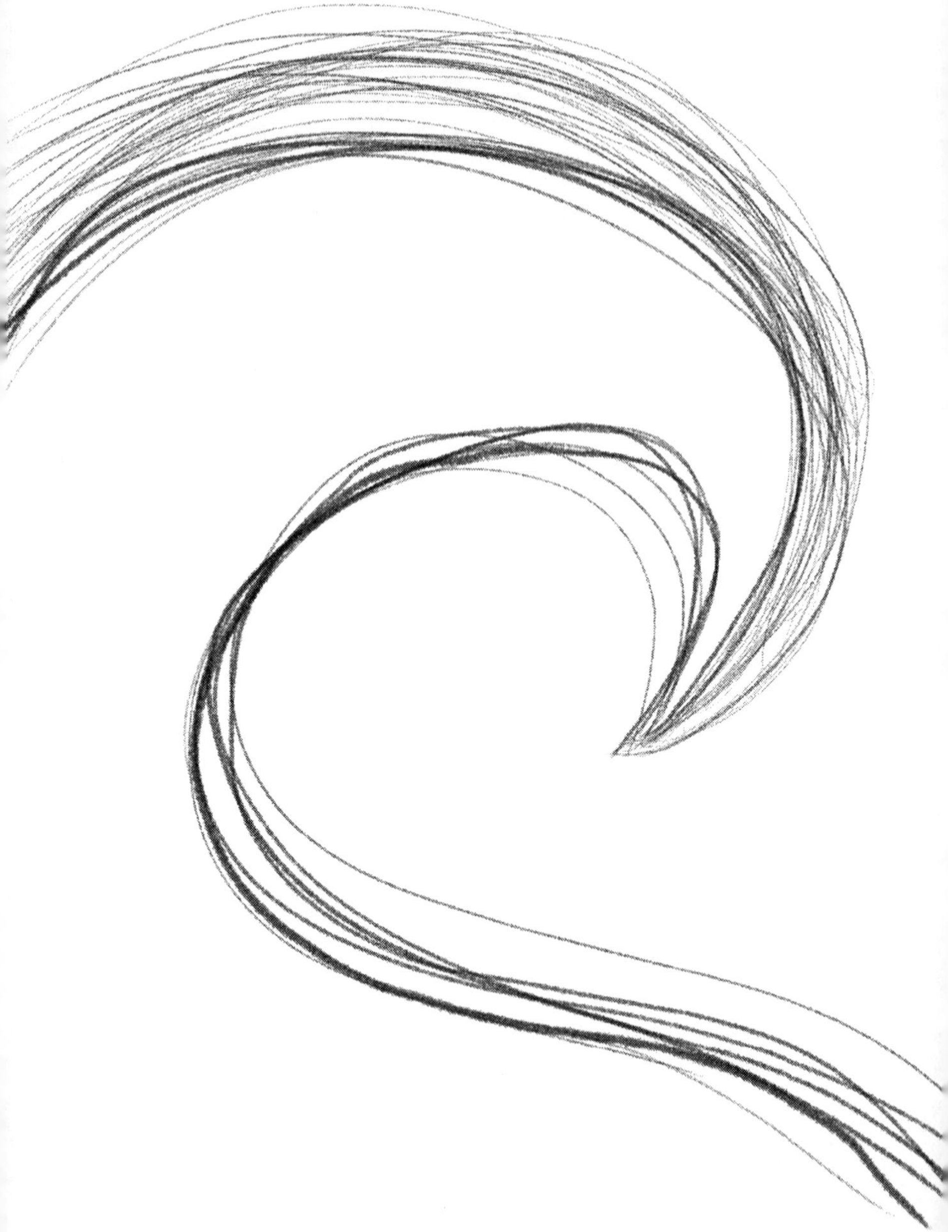

RUSH

home was no longer a place
it was a feeling
that only existed
in the rush of salt water

// © b. gurr

S T A R S

have you ever
had your
    s
      t
        a
          r
            s
f u c k e d
into alignment

// © b. gurr

251

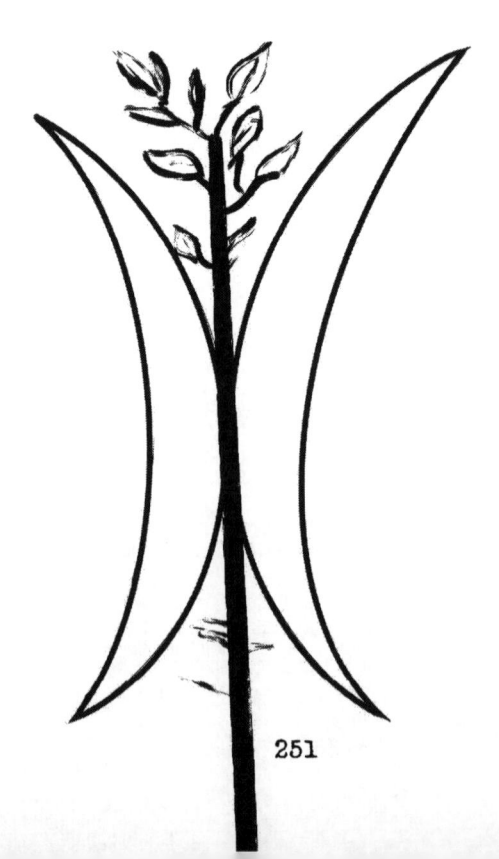

HALF

half a soul? hey baby me too

half my body strong as bamboo

half sag in my sun half cap too

my faces count 'em up one two

a fire sign, gemini is my moon

// © b. gurr

TITANIC

fill my lungs with salt water
let peace drift over me

be my guest
sit & stare

floating on a door
to all your secret places

this life isn't cutting it
let's go everywhere

// © b. gurr

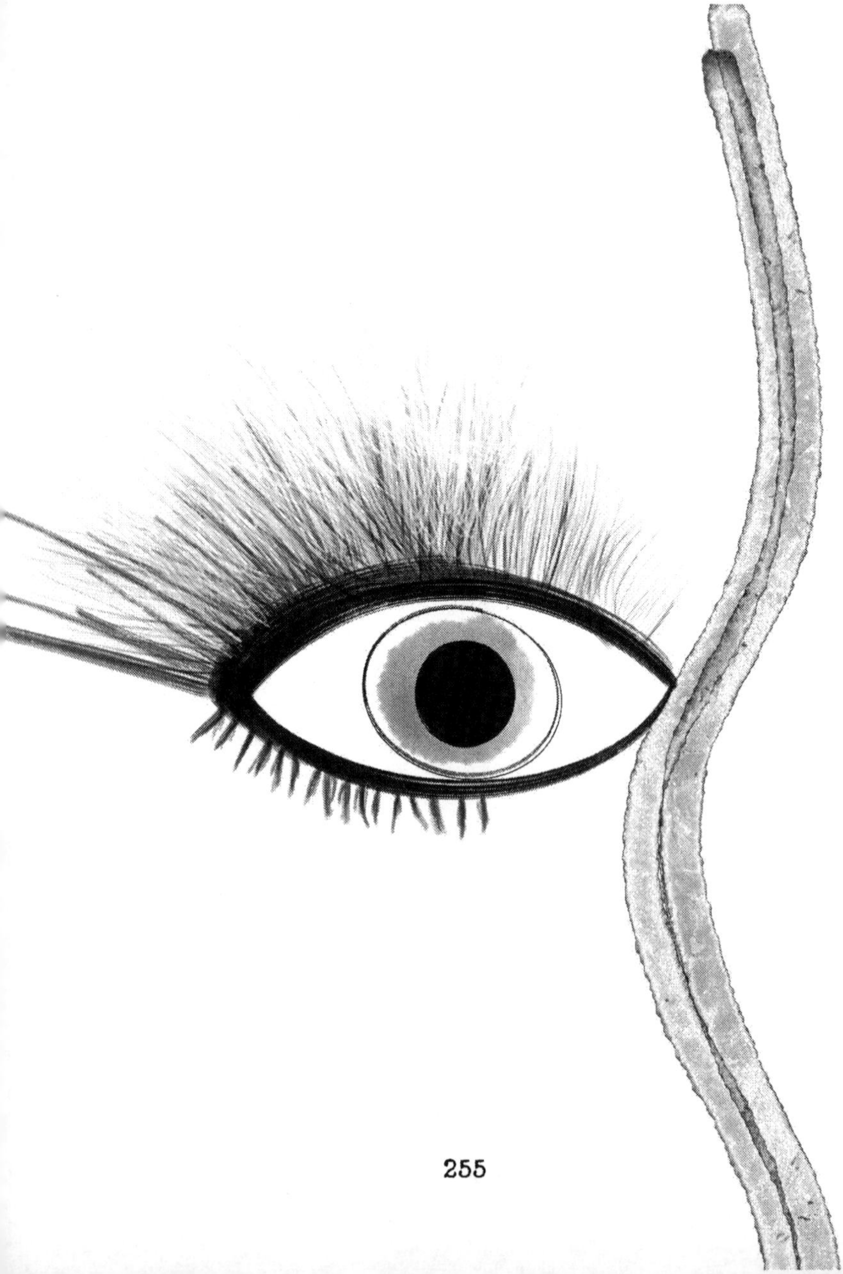

SOUL

eye of the storm
unfolding blossom
i see your soul
in both anomalies often

// © b. gurr

COEXIST

driving into the eye of the storm
all but that bright spot look forlorn
it ain't that cold
but i wouldn't call it warm
clouds so thick they look like swarms
of dust or stars that lost their form
but aren't we all just a storm
of stars or forms
of h2o but really ain't
that all that same
like the place
which we all came
from & still exist
if your mind ain't been twisted
by society & all of which it consists
can't let these storms phase us
just remember this
remain in gratitude, grow in bliss
the age of apologists
are over now we stand together & insist
that for life & loves sake that we coexist
before the storm or in the midst
cause at the end after the mist
the light dances out & kissed
the sky & the rain, tying a bow
reminding us all to glow
& give each other room to grow
to be every colour in the rainbow

// © b. gurr

L O S E

do you know what it feels like
to have him forever
tucked away in plain sight
but lose him at every sun rise

do you know what it feels like
to have love forever
unafraid to shine bright
but lose it at every moon rise

// © b. gurr

RAINBOWS

blue for all those times
they left without a word

red for all the words
that should have gone unsaid

orange for the hope
that ensues each morning

green for the ignorance
that was bliss; was

yellow for the soul
that is lonely

violet for the passion
that overflows into valleys

unbothered & wasted
her tears paint rainbows

// © b. gurr

WARNING

S I G N

baby what's your sign
oh you like games let's play
i can tell that's your thing
hold up can't you see

this scar down my spine
holds more stories than i could say
my sign is bright it says warning
so consider yourself warned by me

golden i spit fire
stars & earth in my veins
sun my goddess love my moon rising
as for water i belong to the sea

// © b. gurr

F L O O D

& all the reasons i ever loved you
came flooding back
when you whispered my name
with tears in your throat
but you left me all the same
wearing your shadow like a coat
choking in the flood
carrying your blood

& all the reasons i ever loved you
came flooding back
when your green abyss
made an endless pool
filled my darkness
hopelessly a fool
so let me drown
beneath this crown

& all the reasons i ever loved you
came flooding back
but just to my mind
cause they never left my soul
so don't be cautious, don't be kind
that sort of thing can take its toll
keeping my heart nude
it won't need rescued

// © b. gurr

DESTINED

a product of your sin
you thought
i was destined
toward doom
but wait this just in
or not
i was destined
for the moon
somewhere nearby or within
real thot
i was destined
to bloom

// © b. gurr

GOODNIGHT

'kiss her goodnight!'
echoed from jupiter to mars

'kiss her goodnight!'
whispered the willow to the ground

'kiss her goodnight!'
sang the mud to the marsh

'kiss her goodnight!'
howled the fox to the hound

'mornings are never sure'
murmured the worm to the robin

'love is the only cure'
i said to them

// © b. gurr

about b.

b. gurr (she/her) author of 'tuesdays; a poetic anthology of nature' is more than a poet, author, & lyricist. ms. gurr is made up of many parts: a diversability advocate, mama, queer, feminist & multi-dimensional artist. surviving traumas, abuse, living with chronic illnesses & diversabilities, gurr's work transmutes growth from the shadows. her creations evolve from a place of resilience, gratitude, unconditional love & passion to inspire humanity's expansion to heal through art & nature.

connect with b.

b.gurr@kahpublishing.com | www.loveb.me | @lovebdotme
#plantbasedpoetry | #sheranwildly
#thescriptwitch | #poetrymadeart

what else b. is up to:

if you enjoyed this collection
& want to gift a certain chapter
they are published separately as:
tuesdays; mind
tuesdays; body
tuesdays; soul

Made in the USA
Monee, IL
06 August 2020